How to Fight Like a Spy: Strategies that you won't find in any gym

Bryan Keyleader

Copyright © Bryan Keyleader, 2012 (1st Edition)
All rights reserved.

Copyright © Bryan Keyleader, 2015 (2nd Edition)
All rights reserved.

Cover Photo Image Via Wikimedia Creative Commons License

2

Table of Contents

Introduction 5

Tactical preparation............................6

Why you may want to avoid fighting 8

Principles for fights you don't want 10

Why arrogance is your worse enemy...............13

Why spies don't want to fight 17

The common denominator in a fight 20

Things that you can't learn in a gym 22

Why gravity and balance are important 26

Fights against groups.....................................28

How to escape from a robbery alive 31

How to escalate a fight....................................34

4

Introduction

Movies have popularized some of the most famous martial arts in modern days, but are they really related to real life survival when it comes to espionage? A spy must fight for survival in the quickest way he can and, for this reason, strategies tend to be more important than techniques when it comes to escaping alive, especially when you intend to avoid fights and not enter them.

Although taking into account strategies to fight in a dangerous environment, this is a book created to be used by people dealing with criminality in a daily basis and for self-defense purposes only. You will learn not only how hot escape confrontation with weapons in the safest way possible, but also gangs. Besides, it's a book dedicated to the average citizen as well as self-defense instructors, and based on street survival skills.

Tactical preparation

If things go wrong, horribly wrong, you must know how many exits are available, which exit to choose from, and which reaction promotes better results and increases chances of survival. If you want to be prepared for combat, forget all the pretty moves from the latest spy movies and get ready for the ugliest. These are the best advices:

- A small knife's razor inside your wallet, next to the paper-dollars, because a metal detector can't show it with precision and can be used as a decoy when preparing to give the money to the agressor, as well as easily grabbed between the index finger and thumb, to be used as a claw;

- A belt with a hidden thin wire inside it, strong enough to cut a man's throat. This is specially effective for women to avoid rape;

- Poisonous needles with shiny metal heads stuck inside the wallet, because while looking as decorative items can also help you hurt badly (or even kill) a group of attackers with just one touch, even while you're being punched and kicked. To learn how to create them, you may want to read about south american tribes in the amazonian jungle, or the tribal tactics of the Indonesian. But, basically, it's the same principle as the bite of a snake. You just have to put the needles in a hot mixture of snake poison. There are many with paralyzing effects;

- Small powder bags (or pepper bags) hidden inside your socks. They can be used to blow the dust at people's eyes when things go bad and you want to avoid getting hit in the first seconds, or to stop them as well. Pepper-spray has basically the same effect. But most of the times you may not have time to get it, which is why having the same content next to your feet may me more suitable when you're facing danger.

Why you may want to avoid fighting

Even though the previous examples are practical for common citizens, they're not for spies, which most of the times can't carry any weapons with them. Besides, you can avoid fights with the following principles:

- You want to build trust with the group you're in;

- You can measure and predict behaviors according to emotional reactions. Basic knowledge on body language can save your life. For example, contraction of the body showing some tension, exaggerated laughs and hands on top of your shoulder, are to be seen as warnings of danger. But know as well that, the one showing delays in his verbal reactions towards what you say, is showing inner opposition.

Other signs of opposition include...

- Fixed observation;

- Lack of hand movements;

- Avoidance, regarding facing another person with the body;

- The need to prove a friendship with encouraging words.

When seeing these situations, you must gain distance and ask questions that allow you to predict and be prepared to what may happen.

Principles for fights you don't want

A fight is very much like a chess game, reason why so many martial arts masters admire games of strategy. It is full of interactions with repetitive patterns, in which movements can only be predicted from the first attitude if a player has enough experience in fighting different opponents. In fact, the ability to predict a movement within a fight is proportional to the gap in experience between fighters. Professional fighters know it, and that's why they always try to make their opponents predictable by forcing them to react in a certain way. Mohammed Ali is one of the best examples in recent history, and Bruce Lee made himself the second great example by extensively studying and following this boxer's principles. But movies aren't honest when portraying a hero winning at the last minute with an unpredictable reaction. There aren't any heroes in a fight and many people have only realized this fact when they paid their trust in a black belt with their own life or, in the best cases, weeks in a hospital's bed.

There are thousands of stories about good martial artists ending up beaten, stabbed and shot by people that they've underestimated.

The problem I've always encountered with martial artists and their teachers, is that it tends to promote quite a lot of arrogance. But arrogance hides stupidity. And that's why sometimes those people challenge individuals with less knowledge than them and end up being severely beaten.

A martial artist is, as the name says, an expert in an art. And art is a group of movements within a certain field of expression. Martial artists can train as much as they want, but they can never replace or perfectly reproduce danger in a street. You cannot train in a gym having to fight when you're afraid to die, when your teeth are broken after a punch or when someone, that you didn't know that was there, knocks you out. And these are the most common situations.

I've had Krav Maga students and instructors asking me to train them, because one thing is to know the techniques and practice them as if you were inside a movie, and another completely different thing is trying to apply them after being punched in the face, while being afraid or in a situation you can't possibly control, like multiple attackers coming at you randomly. It was this psychological training that these arrogant individuals lacked the most, and it was only after practicing with me that they gained back their necessary humbleness and proper awareness.

Why arrogance is your worse enemy

Arrogance is definitely the worse enemy of any expert in fighting. And even I am not immune to that. Because, last time I entered a fight against a taxi driver, and took him to the floor easily, I didn't expect to suddenly have 10 stopping to attack me. It was my experience in strategy that saved me, not techniques. I had to radically change my attitude from the one of a winner to the one of a survivor, or I would surely lose. In fact, almost every single great fighter I met, ended up in hospital after a street fight, because they assumed the winner's attitude from beginning to end. They never thought that they may had to survive, not win. So, they beat one guy, two guys, and then the third hits them with a rock or stick when they least expect.

There are situations in which individuals beat 6 or 7 attackers at the same time. But they're extremely rare and must be analyzed in strategy, not techniques. In all these situations I've heard about, the winner had a very good strategy because he knew well, from personal experience, how street fighters think. He wasn't necessarily trusting his dojo advices. And I'm including here stories about Karate and MuayThai Instructors as well.

There's more into a fight than what we can see or is thought to believe. Native Americans have a saying about this: Two wolves prepare for a fight. One is evil, full of anger and hate; the other is good, full of joy and faith. Who will win? The answer is the one you feed.

I will illustrate this with the story of one of my instructors. I trained him well as a survivor. But he gained arrogance after becoming instructor and having his own students. So, he decided to challenge another instructor for a fight, even though I always insisted that what I was teaching was for survival not competitions.

He lost the fight by points and easily. But, when I watched the video, I noticed something very interesting. In that stick fight, my student was always hitting hard in the head of his opponent, while his opponent was basically touching him many times with his stick every time that happened. He even broke the first stick in his head the first time he hit him.

Do you really think that if those sticks didn't had rubber around them and there were no head gears, my student would lose? No, because after one strong hit to the head, and especially after a person breaks a stick in your had, you have no idea of what to do next, that, if you don't hit the floor unconscious; and that't the illusion of wearing a mask when practicing filipino martial arts.

Thanks to that video of the competition, now the instructor that won has more students and my student has less, because people follow what they see, not what they know. I gained the reputation of one of the best experts in self-defense, but after I left the country, the student replacing me became too arrogant and lost it.

Arrogance is something I can't really teach about or control. My students tend to gain it easily because, after practicing with me, they can beat lots of people that they thought before that they couldn't, like national champions, and then wrongly assume that they're invincible and what applies to one context applies to all. Fighting to survive and to win by points are completely different fields of study. If you practice martial arts, you must understand this difference well, and not expect what you're not being trained for.

Why spies don't want to fight

Do you know why most spies don't want to fight? Because they are trained in martial arts that aren't suitable to survive, only fight, and they know it. They know that they can get killed if they try any jujitsu or kravmaga tactics on a criminal or another spy. Besides, there are many myths about how martial arts begun to attract students and most of these myths are false. And this applies to filipino martial arts as well. However, you may never know the truth, because the Portuguese and Spanish martial arts are disappearing, while the Filipino martial arts, actually based on the fighting exercises of these countries, are rapidly growing around the world, thanks to movies.

The world of martial arts is so complex that, searching for the truth, is like finding gold in a trashcan. It's extremely difficult to find anyone that knows what he's really talking about. But there are some hints that can help you, at least, choose a good instructor, independently of which martial art you choose:

- An ex-prisoner, ex-criminal or ex-gang-member;

- Someone that has faced hand-to-hand combat in war, and specially knife combat;

- Someone that is a bodyguard;

- Someone that has trained self-defense in Russia;

- Someone that is always chosen by other Instructors to add knowledge. Because these Instructors need to learn as well, but they won't choose anyone, and they know exactly who can offer them more valuable information.

My students always assumed I was a spy, but they never tried to understand what makes me a good instructor. The reason is that I basically fit in all the previous items. I'm an ex-gang member and I've faced knife-combat many times. I wasn't a body guard but trained with them and trained them as well, and trained spies. And, I didn't train in Russia but trained with Russians and Chinese. I didn't went to war but my father, which is a veteran and was in hand-to-hand combat with his enemy, used to beat me hard all my life, until the day I he started to be afraid I might kill him if he did it again. And I was also always chosen by other Instructors from different martial arts to improve their knowledge. This happened in Europe, the Philippines and China as well.

The common denominator in a fight

Nobody that understands about fighting wants to spend energy in a fight, especially if it represents a risk to physical integrity. For this reason, these individuals know that a fight starts in the emotional level and turns into physical only under specific circumstances: To assimilate authority, to prove something, to escape or to kill. In any of these given situations, there's an emotional interexchange occurring, in which we're seen as a target for one common reason. If that reason is managed well, it is possible to invert the situation to our advantage. It basically concerns the principle of cause and effect. The target is an effect for some reason, usually not easily perceived in the environment. But the elimination of fear is the most common cause. So, if having the aggressor fearing becoming a victim, we can invert the situation of who is cause or effect.

The truth is that the most vicious people are actually cowards. They only choose those that they assume they can beat. And, if you can find a coward, you can also find a traitor, which is why when you beat the leader of a gang, you may see the rest running away.

Generally speaking, finding a purpose for the attack occurring helps in judging the most suitable reaction, which may vary according to your relation to the attacker or attackers.

Your main purpose, however, should always be to leave untouched from a scene.

Many people that have known me, wonder how I never get hurt in a fight, because they assume the same attitude in all their fights. They think they must fight every single time, and by thinking in such away, they actually suppress the fear of being beaten, which, when under stress, will control their thoughts and ability to react efficiently.

Things that you can't learn in a gym

When in a confrontation, I have less than a second to judge my reaction, and that reaction will determine everything else. If I decide not to attack, the other person may assume that as cowardice, so that less than a second must include his reaction to my reaction, which in chess is called thinking two or three moves in advance. In fact, that's why most martial arts have forms and boxing has sequences. But, if the situation suddenly changes, if one more or ten more people enter suddenly into the quarrel, I need to measure their reaction as well. Sometimes, they are there to make sure you are beaten, other times they are there to make sure the fight doesn't have to occur, but most of the times they are there as witnesses, because they actually want to see a fight happening, most people want to see blood and violence. I've been in several situations in which people actually wanted to see me fight, but when I started beating the other guy, they would stop me. In other words, they were there to see me being beaten or take the other person's side if things didn't occur as they expected.

Actually, most of the times, people grabbed me, not the attacker, because they assumed I have a higher potential to beat the other person. However, when this happens, the attacker gains a huge advantage to attack me, simply because I won't beat the person putting himself in front of me. And that's why a fight is much more complicated than people assume. If I'm beating a guy and a woman puts herself in front of me to grab me, what can I do? I was once in a fight with a guy, when after beating him his girlfriend put herself in front of me to stop me. I did, not to beat her, and in that precise moment two guys came from behind me when I least expected. And that's something gym training will never prepare you to, but may cost your life.

This is also why I don't trust martial arts that focus merely in one type of mindset. A good martial art, teaches about how to have a flexible reaction and a sharp awareness, more than anything else. In other words, you have to really mix the arts. That's why mixed martial artists know how to fight. It's not what they train that makes them good, but the fact that, the more options you have, the better.

In all my experiences, I've noticed that the agressor is usually someone arrogant and stupid. People that aren't arrogant and stupid, but know how to fight, never become an agressor, because they have a different mindset. And this means that, when you face an agressor, you must really think carefully but fast, about what to do. Unfortunately, when people are too stupid and arrogant, they can only be stopped when killed. And that's what happens when you kick the head of a guy several times but he keeps coming back for more.

I never thought of myself as a violent person, but I've been horrible several times in my life, with people that couldn't be stopped and argued with. If you do an arm lock on a person to talk to him or her, but this person tries to bite your leg, then things will have to get very nasty. The same happens when you clearly state that you don't want to fight, and the other individual takes that as him being the strongest and having a chance to beat you. In these situations, I'm actually more afraid of myself than the fight, I'm afraid I may kill the other person when punching his head against the concrete, and I'm also afraid to kill him with his own knife and end up in jail for the rest of my life.

Why gravity and balance are important

The only thing you can't avoid is gravity and, therefore, all actions can be predicted following this simple principle. This means, for example, that a thrown object can cause a person to move to a specific point in space, where your reaction can occur with minimum resistance. When dealing with an inexperienced attacker, this can be enough to break his kneecap with a strong kick. But, when such reaction isn't enough, the throat, the eyes, the ribs and the groin, are the next parts to follow, while the head, being the center of coordination of the body, must be hit with a sharp object, if, and only if, killing is an option. That's actually how police officers think when trying to arrest people in a mob.

The problem with many self-defense tactics is related to the basic fact that, the victim isn't ready to kill someone while the aggressor always is. Most of the aggressions and murders of policemen come from the fact that neither they are.

Taking this issue into account, we can disregard more than 90% of the self-defense programs out there. If you can't kill an animal with your teeth, you can't kill a person with your hands. It's as simple as that. If you keep beating a person down and he keeps coming up, you'll either kill him on purpose or by accident; otherwise he'll kill you.

Not only killing isn't an option for the civilized mind, but it also compromises anyone with professional training.

Nevertheless, the more you focus in stealing the balance of the other individual, the more you can diminish the aggression level you have to apply on him. This is why movements seen in aikido and jujitsu, among other similar martial arts, can be effective in self-defense, if applied, not to win a fight, but to control the opponent or opponents' balance.

Fights against groups

When dealing with a group, you need to focus on the master-mind, which makes the group act as one single organism with one active brain, and that's the leader. The leader commands the group's actions, while the group stimulates the leader's emotions. So, being unexpected and ahead of a leader's decisions is the safest reaction to have in these situations. At this point, the most unexpected reactions include...

- The weakest member in the group being caught and used to stop the rest of the group;

- The leader being knocked out;

- Losing control over a victim.

While the first two reactions demand some level of experience, the third is based on triangular repositioning.

The worst thing you can do, when reacting against a group, is to play Chuck Norris, trying to beat everyone from inside a circle they end up creating on you.

Triangular movements are safer. Triangular movements can be learned in Filipino and Malay Martial arts, even though Bruce Lee has exhaustively mentioned its application in Jun Fan Jeet Kune Do. It consists in imagining an interconnection of triangles among you and your opponents to move yourself strategically according to their movements.

Movies show logical reactions that can only apply in coordinated and repeated training, but to fight a group, you cannot trust your mind or the instruction of a martial arts teacher. Here, everything is about logic in space, which means you must think about the fight as a chess game.

As an example for this, I will mention Portuguese fencing. It looks so easy that even a six year old child can learn it, because it's based more on strategy than techniques. The Portuguese were always a minority in wars against countries with three times or more soldiers. However, they managed to win in all invasions from Spain, England

and France, being the only European country that Napoleons' army couldn't invade, the oldest global empire in history and the oldest European State. Even nowadays, practitioners of this art, following ancient principles for training, try to achieve the highest level possible, by defeating as many opponents as they can, usually from four to ten. And some have won European competitions, against practitioners of other martial arts.

The same applies to the history of the Philippines, where fighting strategies based on blades made them nearly invincible to many invasions with firearms, including the Spanish colonization.

Repositioning yourself with triangular movements also includes forcing the group to move according to your wishes. For this purpose, as in modern days you can't bring a sword with you, you can use a belt, a rock, coins, or any other objects, to be used and thrown, and make sure the group is moving towards where you want them.

How to escape from a robbery alive

Knowing how to escape a person with a gun requires specific understandings that usually only hunters know. For example, escaping in an S-line makes it difficult to aim at the target. A rabbit that constantly changes direction, often escapes alive from the hunter, but also a rat escapes from a lizard by using this same principle. Besides, barriers, such as trees or walls, can block shots.

As for the principles on how to disarm a person, they're usually based on criminal psychology. For example, self-questioning, or self-doubt, distract the aggressor from his target. And it's a fact that thought and actions don't blend well together, especially in men. Even though in these moments a trigger may be pressed by accident, a distraction taking into account both principles mentioned provides more chances to react and escape alive when this is the only option available.

Know also that, when dealing with multiple individuals, lack of logic grants much more chances of escaping than logical behaviors, as only logical reactions are expected and predicted. The more time you spend in a fight, the less chances you have to escape. So, what's the best thing you can say to a thief pointing a knife at you in the street? "You want to rob me with a cop looking at us?"; Or, while shouting loudly to some random people a few steps away from you, you can say: "Hey guys, can you please come here! I forgot my wallet and I need to give some money to this guy!"; Then, don't wait for his brain to rethink in what to do next, while him, or his group, think, you should simply move out.

I've used these strategies to escape robberies along with friends, and nothing happened. But, you can also take an opposite approach and say: "Sure! Come with me to that coffee shop because I need to take a piss and then I help with whatever you want! Come on! Or, wait here! It is up to you!". It can work as well. Or even: "You want to take my money? I just lost my job and you want to take my money? What should I say to my kids when arriving home today without food? Tell me?".

I have some friends that use the last approach all the time, and usually works, because, ironically, robbers respect hardworking people, that can make them remember their own family. It's the rich they hate the most, and that's why in Brazil they kidnap and even kill rich people after robbing them.

To understand these principles better, you may want to research about the stories people tell in Brazil regarding how they escaped alive. Because, real life has much more details into it, than what movies and self-defense instructors can think about showing you. Most of what I learned about how to escape alive came from the study about people that actually did, under very life and death threats.

How to escalate a fight

A fight includes a combination of elements that can apply in different levels and perspectives. In fact, only the most inexperienced minds focus obsessively on techniques in quantity.

These are the levels:

- Level 1 – Emotions and arguments;

- Level 2 – Blocking (Preferably with weapons and other objects);

- Level 3 – Movements and balance;

- Level 4 – Attacks

The level of attack is put here in last place, because it must be executed in a precise way, which requires a certain amount of training. "I fear not the man who has practiced 10,000 kicks once, but I fear the man who has practiced one kick 10,000 times", said Bruce Lee.

Even though this information has been widely suppressed in the last century, the most effective blows in the human body include medical principles that are seen as the basis of ancient Shaolin kung fu (not the modern artistic style), Okinawan karate (not the modern sport style) and the KGB systema (not the one being spread around the world at the moment for self-defense purposes).

One of the common things in which these arts agree with, consists in thinking about the attack as internal instead of external. This means attacking the kidneys, the heart and the throat more than the head or stomach.

The whole structure of this strategy seems to be imperceptible even to those practicing its most modern reminiscences, such as the different forms in Kempo, because there isn't any technique that can be effective by itself, but only when combined in a specific strategic combination of movements. Shorinji Kempo, for example, doesn't look impressive in any way, seems simple and boring to train, but is responsible for cleaning Japan from its criminal gangs after world war 2, and its fighters can easily confront two to three opponents, and also fight on the floor. But in karate, the amount of hand-techniques, that makes it as difficult to learn as complex to understand, has this same intention. Some of the most efficient, include using one of your fingers in a specific position.

Objects that can produce the same effect include a pen, car keys, and even a coin. People often laugh when I say that the coin is the most practical and effective tool to fight with in modern days, because they think the coin is the weapon. But the real effectiveness comes from how you hold a coin and which movements you use it with. One example would be to hold the coin between index finger and thumb; then throw blows in diagonal angles towards the neck as well as temples. Another example would be to use it to hit the ribs.

If you choose to wear a nail between index and middle finger, then the typical boxing punch in a direct line will be more effective. Just remember that, for each object, a specific movement, as well as strategy, is required, and that's why in Kung Fu techniques are understood during the training with weapons. In fact, you should know that, while westerners enjoy practicing taichi inside a class, Chinese prefer to practice it alone, outdoors, with a long sword.

If you practice the use of common objects in a fight, you'll be more prepared than any civilian, because while a knife can't pass airport detectors, pens, pencils and coins, among many other objects that may be used in a fight, can.

Soldiers in ancient times would not use helmets and heavy armory when attacking villages, unless they knew that a farmer, using simple and common farming tools, could kill at least one soldier with one single blow. Farmers may have not been prepared with war strategies, but nearly all of the weapons we see today in martial arts came from realizing that farming tools could be used as weapons.

The suppression of knowledge and highly misleading movies about spy fighting, don't allow people to understand that, nowadays, we have much more deadly objects than before. Maybe not as big, but who uses swords and spears anyway? Apart from what was mentioned, a person must know that, while avoiding confrontation provides more opportunities to escape, drawing attention is sometimes the best choice, but in any case, subtlety and pragmatic creativity have a major role in our protection.

Printed in Great Britain
by Amazon